M000192205

98 REASONS
TO THANK
JIMMY CARTER

98 REASONS

TO THANK

JIMMY

CARTER

ARTHUR MILNES

POLITICAL HISTORY PUBLISHING
Kingston, Ontario
Canada

98 REASONS TO THANK JIMMY CARTER. Copyright © 2022 by Arthur Milnes. First published by Political History Publishing, Kingston, Ontario, Canada.

Photos courtesy of the following:
pages ii, 29, 39, 53, 69, and 97: Jill Stuckey, National Park Service
pages vi, 45, and 105: Habitat for Humanity
pages 7, 15, 23, 27, 36, 73, and 95: Library of Congress
pages 19, 25, and 47: The Carter Center
page 57: U.S. Navy
page 101: the Jimmy Carter Presidential Library and Museum
pages 103 and 121: the author

Designed by Steven Seighman

ISBN: 978-1-7780640-0-5

First Edition: February 2022

98 REASONS

TO THANK

JIMMY CARTER

INTRODUCTION

Jimmy Carter turns 98 this year.

He was the 39th president of the United States.

And of all the U.S. presidents, he has lived the longest.

But there's a whole lot more to Jimmy Carter.

Let's recall a few things he's been and done as we anticipate his birthday on October 1, 2022.

Hold your breath. Ready? Let's go!

James Earl Carter has been a poet, a nuclear scientist, a farmer, a novelist, a painter, a fisher, a carpenter, a winemaker, a Sunday school teacher, a memoirist, a hunter, a peacemaker, a U.S. Naval officer, a Grammy Award winner, a radical, a conservative, a Georgian, an American, a citizen of the world, an environmentalist, a husband to Rosalynn for 76 years, Billy's brother, Miss Lillian's son, a father, a grandfather, a great-grandfather, and a winner of the Nobel Peace Prize.

Pause for a break.

Rested? Let's continue.

He's been a builder of homes for the poor; a slayer of

disease in Africa; a friend of the Queen and of popes, presidents, and prime ministers; a fan-friend of Bob Dylan, the Allman Brothers, Willie Nelson, and Eddie Vedder; a pain in the butt for the U.S. presidents who followed him; a role model to millions all the same; and, above all else, the best of what we can be.

Some today call him "Jimmy." Others call him "Mr. President." The odd old-timer in Georgia still calls him "Governor." At church he's plain old "Brother Jimmy." A lot of Republicans (and more than a few Democrats) still don't have a clue what to call him.

Me? I call him a hero, the one and only. The Man From Plains.

He's been with us so long that I fear we risk taking him for granted. That just won't do.

So, taking a few pages from his life and example, I decided to write this tribute to Jimmy for his 98th birthday.

This is for my readers and fellow Jimmy fans. It has to remain a secret before October 1: I don't want to spoil the surprise. Herein you'll find 98 reasons to thank Jimmy Carter.

Happy 98th birthday, Jimmy.

And most of all: Thank you.

Some of the proceeds from this book will be donated to a cause dear to Jimmy Carter's heart: Habitat for Humanity.

I know he'll like that.

HE'S NEVER SMOKED.

Jimmy can't stand smoking. His presidential administration declared war on this dirty—and dangerous—habit. They got really serious—like, *really* serious—about cutting smoking rates across the country. Jimmy's daddy, sisters, and brother all smoked, and they all died of pancreatic cancer. Jimmy says he's been spared their fate because he's never been a smoker. He truly set an example for American youth tempted to light that first cigarette. Jimmy also understands addiction and has been a beacon for smokers who want to quit.

For caring about health: Thank you, Jimmy.

HE COMFORTED ELVIS IN THE KING'S FINAL DAYS.

The king of rock'n'roll was in a sad state in the weeks prior to his death in 1977. One day, while particularly stoned, Elvis was peeved because a friend of his had been charged with a criminal offense. So, the King called the White House, hoping President Carter would issue a preemptive pardon for his buddy. Jimmy took the call. He gently and graciously talked Elvis down.

"Elvis Presley's death deprives our country of a part of itself. He was unique and irreplaceable," the Man From Plains said when the King died, only a few days after they chatted on the phone.

Thank you, Jimmy.

HE MADE CRAFT BEER POSSIBLE.

Before Jimmy was president, going back to the days of the Great Depression, Americans weren't allowed to brew their own beer. So for decades America and Americans were known worldwide for brewing and consuming arguably the worst beer on earth. Jimmy changed all that. On October 14, 1978, he signed into law a restoration of the rights of his country's citizens to brew and sell their own suds. Today there are around 9,000 craft breweries in the States. Beer tastes better (does it ever!), Americans are happier, and thousands are now employed in an ever-growing industry.

Thank you, Jimmy.

HE MARRIED ROSALYNN.

The future president fell in love with his sister Ruth's best friend, Rosalynn Smith. She was—and still is—beautiful. They married when Jimmy was 21 and Rosalynn 18. This year they celebrate their 76th wedding anniversary. In marrying Rosalynn, Jimmy helped make it possible for her, as first lady, to advocate for the mentally ill and for prisoners and caregivers of seniors and to oppose the death penalty. Millions have been impacted by her efforts in these areas and through her countless other selfless campaigns. Had he not asked her out on a date all those years ago….

Thank you, Jimmy (and Rosalynn).

HE'S THE WORLD'S COOLEST BAPTIST.

Jimmy goes to church every Sunday. His denomination has always been Baptist. Brother Jimmy, born again decades ago, has bucked the right-wing and sometimes divisive stereotype of American Evangelicals. He accepts people for who and what they are. In his view, religion should unite, not divide. "My faith demands that I do whatever I can, wherever I am, whenever I can, for as long as I can with whatever I have to try to make a difference," he once said. Words to live by.

Amen to that, and: Thank you, Jimmy.

HE AND ROSALYNN ARE ERADICATING A TERRIBLE DISEASE.

When Jimmy and Rosalynn left the White House, 3.5 million people in the developing world annually were afflicted with Guinea worm disease—an awful, parasite-borne reality with worms as long as three feet growing in the body, crippling millions and causing pain and misery difficult to imagine. Jimmy decided to act. It took him and Rosalynn and their Carter Center teams about two decades to slay this beast. Thanks to Jimmy, those 3.5 million cases shrank to only 14 in 2021. Take that, Guinea worm!

Thank you, Jimmy.

HE MADE BOB DYLAN FEEL AT HOME.

America's ever-reluctant poet laureate is as restless and personally guarded as they come. But in the 1970s, while Bob Dylan was touring with The Band, Jimmy invited him over to the Governor's Mansion in Georgia after a show. While other politicians had tried to get a piece of the troubadour's fame, Jimmy was just his usual humble self.

How did it feel for Bob Dylan? "When I first met Jimmy, the first thing he did was quote my songs back to me," Dylan later said. "He put my mind at ease by not talking down to me and showing me he had a sincere appreciation of the songs I had written."

Thank you, Jimmy (and Bob).

8

HE MADE RUTH BADER GINSBURG A JUDGE.

Supreme Court Justice Ruth Bader Ginsburg was a liberal icon. As tenacious as she was gracious, Justice Ginsburg fought for and advanced equal rights for women. Nominated to the Supreme Court by President Bill Clinton in 1993, RBG was by then a veteran member of the U.S. Court of Appeals. And who put her on that court? President Jimmy Carter, in April 1980. Had he not made such an inspired appointment, would RBG have ever served on the Supreme Court of the United States and made such important contributions to history?

Thank you, Jimmy.

9

HE MADE IT OK TO ADMIT YOU'VE SEEN A UFO.

In 1969, Jimmy reported that he'd seen a UFO. The Man From Plains even told people about it. The sighting took place outside a Lion's Club meeting in a small Georgia town. In reporting what he had witnessed, the future U.S. president joined the thousands who had also reported sightings and were often ridiculed. Jimmy stood by his guns when the incident went public.

"One thing's for sure, I'll never make fun of people who say they've seen unidentified objects in the sky," he said.

Thank you, Jimmy.
(And may you live long and prosper.)

HE PRAYS FOR DONALD TRUMP.

Lots of Christians go to church every week, listen to a sermon, act pious for an hour, and then go on with their un-Christian thoughts and actions the rest of the week.

Not Jimmy. He means what he prays.

While disgusted by former President Donald Trump's policies and personal behavior, Jimmy put his religion first—as difficult as it seems that would have been. Well into the Trump presidency, Jimmy said he was still praying for his successor. Which made many Carter fans cringe.

But it also made Jimmy a true Christian.

Thank you, Jimmy.

HE STOOD BY BROTHER BILLY.

Jimmy's brother Billy was an unforgettable part of the Carter era. He was a proud, beer-swilling Southerner who could guarantee any reporter a homespun quote on a slow news day. Although Billy's antics would often embarrass the president, Jimmy's love for him never waned. He put up with the questions and clamor because he knew Billy suffered from a disease that afflicted millions of Americans: alcoholism. Jimmy stood by his brother and celebrated, along with the whole Carter clan and their friends, when Billy beat the bottle. Billy died in 1988, sober.

Thank you, Jimmy.

12

HE CAMPAIGNED FOR DYLAN THOMAS.

Jimmy has been inspired by Welsh poet Dylan Thomas. "I have had an affinity for Dylan Thomas's poetry, and in my opinion, he is one of the greatest poets of the 20th century," Jimmy has said. "I bought all his books and records and remember reciting his poems to my children until they memorized them." While on a visit to England as president, Jimmy even publicly called for the poet to be recognized—finally—in Poets' Corner in Westminster Abbey. A few years later, a memorial to Jimmy's favorite poet was unveiled in that hallowed place.

Thank you, Jimmy.

HE DIDN'T LIE.

Running for president in 1976, just two years after the Watergate scandal, Jimmy promised the American people he would never lie to them. Cynical big-city news columnists and D.C. politicos made fun of him for that promise. But guess what? Jimmy kept his word. He never lied to the American people.

U.S. Vice President Walter Mondale put it best: "We told the truth, obeyed the law, and kept the peace." Not a bad legacy for any presidential administration.

Can all of those who succeeded him say the same?

Thank you, Jimmy.

14

HE FORGED A LASTING PEACE BETWEEN EGYPT AND ISRAEL.

In September 1978, Jimmy brought the leaders of Israel and Egypt to Camp David to encourage them to make peace with each other. Until then, the two nations had repeatedly fought bloody wars that had cost thousands of lives. Jimmy wouldn't allow either leader to leave without reaching an agreement and kept them at the negotiating table for 13 days that historic September. He insisted they compromise. And so the Camp David Accords were signed. That was 44 years ago, and the peace Jimmy brokered still holds. Countless lives have been spared.

Thank you, Jimmy.

HE HELPED SAVE CANADA'S CAPITAL FROM A NUCLEAR MELTDOWN.

In the early 1950s, Jimmy was a young U.S. Naval officer at the dawn of the Atomic Age. He worked on the earliest atom-powered submarines. When a nuclear reactor near Canada's capital experienced a partial meltdown, Jimmy was ordered to secretly lead a team of American servicemen to help the Canucks fix their reactor. He even entered the damaged reactor building and defied radiation itself. He did get zapped, however, and had radiation in his urine for some months afterward. But thanks to Jimmy and his colleagues, the reactor was repaired and life around Ottawa could go on as usual.

Thank you, Jimmy.

HE WROTE A NOVEL AND INCLUDED A RACY SEX SCENE.

Jimmy is the first president of the United States to write a novel. He published it in 2003. *The Hornet's Nest* is set in Georgia during the American Revolution, and Jimmy had no qualms about including a steamy sex scene.

"He was overwhelmed with a feeling of tenderness and also aroused sexually, which his tight trousers made obvious to both of them," the novelist former president wrote. You get the point. Jimmy even read that scene while appearing on a late-night talk show. The viewers loved it!

Thank you, Jimmy.

— **17** —

HE MADE WALTER MONDALE VICE PRESIDENT.

Until Jimmy came along, presidents sometimes treated their vice presidents with disdain. For the most part, past prezzes didn't seem to want their veeps around them. Jimmy thought that was ridiculous; he knew that a president needed all the help they could get. So he treated his VP, Walter Mondale, as an equal. Anything Jimmy knew, he made sure Walter knew as well. After all, a VP might become president in an instant. Thus it was that the 39th president and his VP turned the vice presidency into an office that mattered. And it remains so to this day.

Thank you, Jimmy.

18

HE WENT TO CUBA.

In 2002, Jimmy became the first president, sitting or past, to visit Cuba since the island's Communist revolution. When Fidel Castro invited Jimmy to come to his country, our hero had one condition: that he be allowed to deliver a speech to the Cuban people calling for their government to finally respect human rights and institute democratic reforms. Castro reluctantly agreed, and the Man From Plains made his speech. Then Fidel took Jimmy to a baseball game: Jimmy threw the first pitch, and thousands of Cubans cheered (he probably had a better pitching arm than Castro).

Thank you, Jimmy.

HE'S AMY'S FATHER.

Amy, Jimmy and Rosalynn's only daughter, was nine when she moved into the White House and became first daughter. She attended D.C. public schools just like regular kids, and her tree house on the White House property became famous. Amy was becoming a teenager when she and her parents left Washington in 1981. She finished high school and college while pretty much keeping to herself to preserve her privacy. Once, however, she got arrested for standing up for what she believed in. She was known in particular for protesting against South African apartheid and the illegal activities of the CIA. Like father, like daughter.

Thank you, Jimmy (and Amy).

HE IMMORTALIZED HIS FAVORITE TEACHER.

While he was growing up in Plains, Jimmy was greatly impacted by his favorite teacher, Miss Julia Coleman. He still maintains that she opened his eyes to a wider world. "Study hard: One of you could become the president of the United States!" she told her students. One of them did just that. Jimmy quoted Miss Julia both in his inaugural address and in his Nobel Peace Prize acceptance speech. Teachers worldwide must have appreciated that. Here's that timeless quote: "We must adjust to changing times and still hold to unchanging principles."

Thank you, Jimmy (and Miss Julia).

Miss Julia Coleman
Principal, inspirational teacher, and superintendent

HE PARDONED VIETNAM WAR DRAFT DODGERS.

During the Vietnam War thousands of young Americans dodged the draft, seeking shelter in countries like Sweden and Canada. Others went underground in the USA. Families were divided, opinions were strong on all sides of the issue, and there appeared very little middle ground. Jimmy, however, wanted the wounds of that terrible war healed, whatever the political cost. On January 20, 1977, his very first day as president, he pardoned all those young people who had fled their families and friends. Many of Jimmy's opponents were angry but the Man From Plains—as always—sought peace and harmony for the country. In doing so, he set America on the path to healing. As we know today, it was the right thing to do.

Thank you, Jimmy.

HE WON THE NOBEL PEACE PRIZE.

Before Jimmy came along, only two U.S. presidents, Teddy Roosevelt and Woodrow Wilson, had ever won the Nobel Peace Prize. In 2002, the good folks in Norway chose Jimmy as that year's recipient of the world's most prestigious award. And Jimmy had earned it: He had fostered peace throughout the world his entire career. "War may sometimes be a necessary evil. But no matter how necessary, it is always an evil, never a good," Jimmy said in his acceptance speech. "We will not learn how to live together in peace by killing each other's children." Wise words.

Thank you, Jimmy.

23

HE GAVE *SATURDAY NIGHT LIVE*'S DAN AYKROYD GREAT MATERIAL TO WORK WITH.

Luckily for *Saturday Night Live* alumnus Dan Aykroyd, Jimmy can laugh at himself. The famed actor's impersonations of President Carter on *SNL* episodes are the stuff of legend. Years later, however, Dan felt a bit guilty about making fun of the Man From Plains. In 2012, when Dan heard that Jimmy and Rosalynn were staying in the Canadian town where Dan lives part-time, the actor sent the couple a case of his Dan Aykroyd wine to enjoy during their stay. "Well, I've earned this," Jimmy said, sporting his famous smile as he held a glass of Dan's wine at dinner.

Thank you, Jimmy (and Dan).

HE BUGGED THE SOVIETS BY PUTTING HUMAN RIGHTS AT THE TOP OF THE WORLD'S AGENDA.

Jimmy became president during the Cold War. Although they had done their best, his predecessors had run out of ideas in trying to convince the communist parts of the world that America's path was the best one. Not Jimmy. Every time he met a Soviet leader, he hit them—in public and in private—where it truly hurt: by pointing out their lack of support for human rights in Russia and around the world.

"Human rights is the soul of our foreign policy because human rights are the very soul of our sense of nationhood," said the Man From Plains. More words to live by.

Thank you, Jimmy.

HE PLACED A PORTRAIT OF DR. MARTIN LUTHER KING JR. IN GEORGIA'S CAPITOL.

Before Jimmy became Georgia's governor, there wasn't a single portrait of an African American on display in the state capitol—and this despite the fact that a quarter of the state's population were African-American! Governor Jimmy changed all that. In 1974, while angry Ku Klux Klan members demonstrated outside, Jimmy oversaw the unveiling of a portrait of the great Dr. King. At long last, in MLK's home state and in her majestic capitol, the late civil rights leader was honored. And he is to this day. And a portrait of the Man From Plains is there, too.

Thank you, Jimmy (and Dr. King).

HE ENCOURAGED AMERICANS TO ROLL UP THEIR SLEEVES AND GET A COVID-19 VACCINATION.

In 2021, at age 96, Jimmy (and Rosalynn) stood up to the anti-vaxxers and rolled up their sleeves to receive a COVID-19 vaccination. (And to give equal credit, former presidents George W. Bush, Bill Clinton, and Barack Obama did the same.) In order to assist in the fight against the virus, the Carters also sent out on social media a picture of themselves wearing masks. You can bet that many of their admirers and friends were inspired to do so, too. Once again, Jimmy and Rosalynn used their prominence to fight for a good cause and help save American lives.

Thank you, Jimmy (and Rosalynn).

HE MADE SOLAR PANELS COOL.

Anticipating the need to battle climate change decades before most people did, Jimmy looked ahead and saw that America had to start doing something about it. He called the press in and showed off the solar panels he'd ordered installed on the White House roof. His idea seemed so "out there" that Ronald Reagan took them down. Boy, was the Gipper wrong! Today, solar power and renewables are not only cool—they're crucial to saving the planet. There are now 375,000 Americans employed in the industry. And the Man From Plains started it all.

Thank you, Jimmy (and the planet thanks you, too).

HE WON A GRAMMY.

Actually, that is incorrect: Jimmy has won *three* of them! Like his friend Elvis, Jimmy is therefore a Grammy king in his own right. He's won a coveted Grammy Award in the best spoken word category after recording his books numerous times. Jimmy took home the miniature gramophone for his volumes *Our Endangered Values: America's Moral Crisis, A Full Life: Reflections at Ninety,* and *Faith—A Journey for All.* He received his first Grammy nomination in the 1990s and his most recent one in 2018. Now millions worldwide can listen to and learn from his words of wisdom.

Thank you, Jimmy.

HE MADE CARDIGANS COOL.

Cardigans were out of fashion by the time Jimmy arrived at the White House. But that didn't stop our hero! Only two weeks into the job, he delivered a nationally televised address about energy conservation while sitting in front of a fire. What was he wearing? You guessed it: a cardigan. And he went on wearing them. They felt good, he looked good—and Mr. Rogers was definitely pleased. Not before, or since, has the cardigan industry had such an effective promoter of their products in the White House.

Thank you, Jimmy.

HE MADE IT POSSIBLE FOR WILLIE NELSON TO SMOKE A DOOBIE ON THE WHITE HOUSE ROOF.

While Jimmy hates smoking, we know that he invited Willie Nelson to perform at the White House and then spend the night. Many years later, Jimmy's son Chip—and this is confirmed by Willie—admitted that he and his father's distinguished musical guest smoked a doobie that night on the White House roof. Although Jimmy was in bed fast asleep when the weedfest took place, you have to give him credit for making that historic event possible. Willie does indeed love to get high, as Ringo says, with a little help from his friends.

Thank you, Jimmy.

ANDY WARHOL'S PORTRAITS OF HIM ARE COOL.

What do Marilyn Monroe, Elvis Presley, Elizabeth Taylor, Jackie O, Debbie Harry, John Wayne, Queen Elizabeth, and the Man From Plains have in common? Andy Warhol, of course. The patron saint of pop art immortalized all of them. Warhol's portrayals of Jimmy are, quite simply, the best. He later gave one to Jimmy and it remains in Atlanta. Others followed. Some say they are the coolest items—next to Jimmy's famous cardigan—in the museum and The Carter Center's collections.

Thank you, Jimmy (and Andy).

HE POPULARIZED PEANUTS.

Jimmy was the first peanut farmer to become president. So it will surprise no one that a special peanut festival is held annually in his hometown. It's called Plains, Peanuts, and a President. Jimmy and Rosalynn always attend. Folks travel from all over America to participate in the festivities. Peanut farmers, and those of us who love eating their products, remain forever in Jimmy's debt for the spotlight he continues to shine on this delicious legume (yes, it's a "legume"!). The National Peanut Board, for example, says about 7,000 American farmers grow peanuts today across 13 U.S. states. Georgia, of course, grows the most peanuts of all.

Thank you, Jimmy.

HE BUILDS HOUSES FOR THE UNDERPRIVILEGED.

After leaving the White House, Jimmy and Rosalynn began a yearly tradition of building houses for the poor through Habitat for Humanity. All these decades later, Habitat reports the couple have personally built, renovated, or repaired almost 4,500 homes across America and around the world! The Man From Plains and his wife hammer nails just like every other volunteer. They even worked on the 100,000th Habitat house. And that felt so good, they worked on number 100,001 as well. Guess where the latter is located? It stands proudly (and fittingly) in Plains, Georgia.

Thank you, Jimmy (and Rosalynn).

HE FIGHTS FOR FREE AND HONEST ELECTIONS.

When Jimmy and Rosalynn are not busy eradicating diseases, they're helping ensure fair elections worldwide. Since he left office, Jimmy and his crew have monitored elections in more than 65 countries. Heck, he even monitored an election in Nepal! One time, Jimmy even confronted government toughs in Panama while they tried to fake a free election by stuffing ballot boxes for a dictator. Super Jimmy jumped on a table and stared them down. "Are you honest, or are you thieves?" he famously shouted in Spanish.

Gracias, Jimmy.

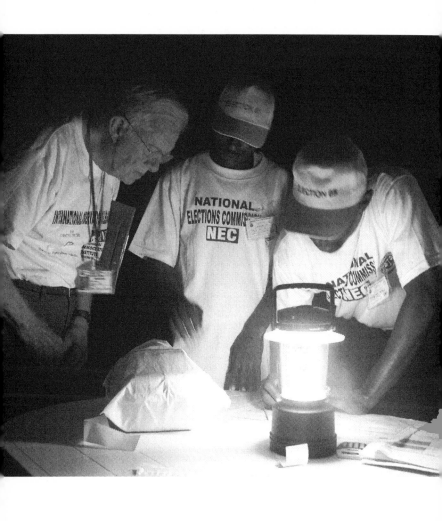

HE PRESERVED THE ALASKAN WILDERNESS.

Not long before he left office, Jimmy crafted a law protecting 104 million acres of Alaska's pristine environment for future Americans. This led to the formation of new national parks, wildlife refuges, and so much more. Today, Jimmy calls this one of his proudest accomplishments from his White House days. We agree. Generations of Americans who have since visited Alaska are in his debt, as will be future generations.

"If we can teach our children to honor nature's gifts, the joys and beauties of the outdoors will be here forever," the Man From Plains once said.

Thank you, Jimmy (and the planet thanks you yet again).

HE CREATED THOUSANDS OF JOBS FOR AMERICAN TRUCKERS AND SAVED CONSUMERS A LOT OF MONEY.

When he was president, Jimmy deregulated the trucking industry. During the 1980s, 500,000 Americans, now free of restrictive government regulations, were able to find jobs as truckers. Let's repeat that: a half million new jobs! There was also a bonus: Shipping costs for American consumers and American companies dropped a great deal. Everyone was a winner.

Except Jimmy. It wasn't until years later that the positive effects of his Motor Carrier Act were felt. Who took all the credit? Ronald Reagan. But today we know whom we really have to thank.

Thank you, Jimmy.

HE NEGOTIATED A NUCLEAR ARMS REDUCTION AGREEMENT WITH THE SOVIET UNION.

Jimmy wanted—and still does—to rid the world of nuclear weapons. On the road to that dream, he and his administration negotiated the SALT II agreement with the Soviets. It wasn't perfect, but it was a beginning. Congress wouldn't pass it, but the boys in Moscow still abided by most of SALT II's terms. When the Man From Plains signed the agreement one day in Vienna, the world was made a bit safer. Jimmy even put up with a kiss from Soviet boss Leonid Brezhnev! Now that was mighty brave.

Thank you, Jimmy.

HE'S ALWAYS BEEN FAITHFUL TO ROSALYNN.

When Jimmy said "I do," he meant it. While other presidents have, shall we say, not always taken their marriage vows to heart (I'm talkin' 'bout you, JFK and WJC), Jimmy has. Rosalynn is the only girl he's ever loved. In July they'll celebrate their 76th wedding anniversary! Amazing. Inspirational. "For 75 years of marriage we've always gone deeper in our love for one another," the Man From Plains said last year when celebrating their 75th anniversary. "I think that's a kind of extraordinary thing. Doesn't happen to very many couples, but it certainly happened to us."

Thank you, Jimmy (and Rosalynn).

HE'S MADE SUNDAY SCHOOL COOL.

Almost every Sunday since leaving the White House, Jimmy has taught Sunday school at his little Baptist church in Plains. People have come from around the USA and across the globe to hear him speak, sometimes 600 on a given week! All told, an estimated 70,000 people have seen Jimmy teach the Gospel in Plains. "We'll never know whether something new and wonderful is possible unless we try," he once told his students. "Let's scratch our heads, stretch our minds, be adventurous! Serve God with boldness, and who knows what wonders the Lord may work."

Amen to that and, yet again: Thank you, Jimmy.

HE NEVER SENT OUR MEN AND WOMEN TO WAR.

Jimmy hates war. During the four years he served as president, he never once sent young Americans off to a foreign war. On his last day in office, a friend and assistant gave him a special plaque displaying a quote from Thomas Jefferson: "I have the consolation to reflect that during the period of my Administration not a drop of the blood of a single citizen was shed by the sword of war."

These words from the Man From Plains are equally profound. "My position has always been, along with many other people, that any differences be resolved in a nonviolent way." Now *that* should be engraved on a plaque and hung in the Oval Office.

Thank you, Jimmy.

HE'S BEEN AROUND LONGER THAN THE QUEEN.

This year, Queen Elizabeth—who knows Jimmy very well—is celebrating 70 years on the British throne. Her Majesty also turns 96 this year. Those are great milestones, for sure, but Jimmy has her beat: He's turning 98 this year. And guess what? Unlike the Queen, he wasn't born into leadership but actually had to get elected to serve as America's head of state.

Still, you have to admit the Queen's pretty cool. The Man From Plains thinks so, too. And they've both put public service ahead of themselves for decades.

Thank you, Jimmy (and Your Majesty).

HE KNOWS HOW TO DRIVE A SUBMARINE.

It's no wonder the U.S. Navy has an atomic submarine called the *USS Jimmy Carter*. As a young U.S. Naval officer at the outset of the Cold War, Jimmy served aboard a submarine called the *SSSK-1*. And he was good at his job. Hyman Rickover, the famed admiral, even had Jimmy return to college to learn the latest in reactor technology. And he excelled at his studies. Why? Perhaps because ever since he was a kid, the Man From Plains had wanted to join the Navy and see the world.

Thank you, Jimmy, for your service.

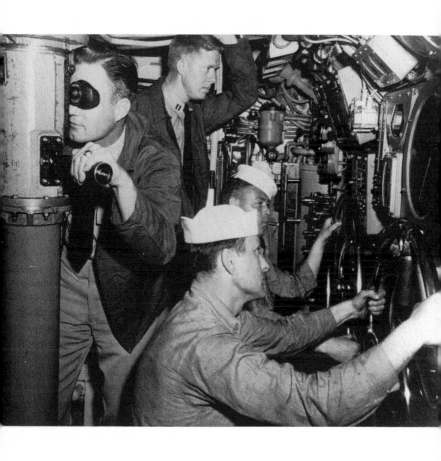

HE'S HAD LUST IN HIS HEART, BUT NOT IN THE OVAL OFFICE.

When he was running for president, Jimmy was interviewed by *Playboy Magazine* and admitted that, despite his happy marriage to Rosalynn, he'd shown lust in his heart over the years. From today's vantage point, that admission is pretty tame! And since then, we've lived through a scandal where a U.S. president showed, well, much more than lust in his heart in the Oval Office. The Man From Plains never sullied the presidency with that sort of conduct. The Man From Plains also proved that *Playboy* was, in fact, more about the articles than the pictures. But that's for another day.

Thank you, Jimmy.

HE'S BEATEN BRAIN CANCER.

Many doctors believed Jimmy's fate was sealed when he was diagnosed with brain cancer in 2015. His melanoma had expanded to his liver and brain. Most thought Super Jimmy was a goner. And he was, after all, 91. The situation looked bleak. But just as the Guinea worms found out, Jimmy loves nothing better than a fight. He gave doctors permission to try out experimental treatments, and thanks to them and through sheer will he defeated cancer itself. He's given hope to millions facing that horrid disease. He never gave up. Neither do they.

Thank you, Jimmy.

HE SHOWED UP THE AYATOLLAH.

Had Jimmy bombed Tehran (as many people wanted him to), the Ayatollah and his henchmen would have killed the Americans they held in captivity. Jimmy wouldn't stand for that, so he did the right thing: He put American lives ahead of his own reelection. And the hostages eventually came home. He even got to meet them in person. The hostage crisis cost Jimmy the election, that's for sure, but his actions showed anything but weakness: They were the sign of a very strong president and a true man of faith—unlike the actions of the religious extremist a world away. In the end, and at great cost to his own political career, the Man From Plains beat the Ayatollah.

Thank you, Jimmy.

HE WROTE A REALLY COOL CHILDREN'S BOOK.

As all parents should, Jimmy told stories to his children before they went to sleep. Later in life he and his daughter Amy published *The Little Baby Snoogle-Fleejer,* a children's book based on a favorite story of theirs. Now countless kids—and their moms and dads—have read this childhood tale. And if Jimmy and Amy's choice isn't the coolest one ever for a "presidential" book, I don't know what is. The illustrations are something else: Amy did those herself. What an incredible team.

Thank you, Jimmy (and Amy).

47

HE SPREADS PEACE AROUND THE WORLD.

Over the years, Jimmy and Rosalynn have visited over 145 countries. In doing so they have brought peace, comfort, understanding, and hope to millions. Jimmy is truly a citizen of the world. People love him everywhere because they know he loves them back. For example, Jimmy and Rosalynn traveled to Canada and helped build 150 Habitat for Humanity homes to mark that nation's 150th birthday in 2017. Countries worldwide owe them a debt of gratitude for the shelter they've provided—literally—for their citizens. They are America's unstoppable goodwill ambassadors.

Thank you, Jimmy (and Rosalynn).

HE WANTS MORE AMERICANS VOTING, NOT FEWER.

Like all well-thinking Americans on both sides of the partisan divide, Jimmy is repulsed by the idea of trying to prevent citizens from voting. Since the 2020 election and even before that, he's called out those, even in his home state of Georgia, who use laws and loopholes to keep citizens—particularly African Americans—from voting. Unlike Donald Trump and his supporters at last year's infamous U.S. Capitol breach, his actions show that he respects democracy. Jimmy too lost a presidential election—but never questioned the results. Voting rights are sacred to him—as they should be to us all.

Thank you, Jimmy.

HE STILL BUGS REPUBLICANS.

For generations of American Republicans, Jimmy has been a curse. He's called them out on a wide range of issues: from gun control and protecting the environment to foreign affairs and, in recent years, their dangerous and divisive embrace of Trumpism and DT himself. That said, he is also fair. He spoke at the official dedication of the George W. Bush Presidential Library in Dallas and crossed the partisan divide to praise the 43rd president. And he has always had enormous respect for former presidents George H.W. Bush, Gerald Ford, and Dwight Eisenhower. For Jimmy, personal integrity trumps (forgive the pun) political party.

Thank you, Jimmy.

50

HE STILL BUGS DEMOCRATS.

Jimmy is consistent. When he sees a wrong, a mistake, or an injustice to correct, he goes into action even if the president du jour is a Democrat. And for years, many Democrats wouldn't even utter Jimmy's name. He didn't care: He fought with Bill Clinton when he thought 42 was wrong and called out Barack Obama when he thought 44 made mistakes. Jimmy wants a better America, and when the going gets tough he disregards partisanship. However, no one will deny he appreciated it when President Joe Biden and First Lady Dr. Jill Biden dropped by Plains to say hello. He still likes Joe.

Thank you, Jimmy.

HE PREVENTED A WAR WITH CENTRAL AND SOUTH AMERICANS OVER THE PANAMA CANAL.

Ronald Reagan used to bring crowds to their feet by proclaiming of the Panama Canal, "We built it, we paid for it, it's ours, and we should tell [the Panamanians] and Co. that we are going to keep it!" Great rhetoric, for sure, but Reagan ignored the fact that the canal was a festering time bomb relative to the millions who lived far south of our border. So Jimmy braved the political heat and negotiated the Panama Canal Treaty. Although Reagan cried foul, the treaty still stands. President Jimmy did the right thing: He walked a few miles in Panamanian shoes and an eventual war was averted.

Thank you, Jimmy.

HE MADE IT CHEAPER FOR AMERICANS TO FLY.

Before Jimmy came along, boarding a plane and flying to enjoy a magical holiday destination was something only rich Americans could afford. This bugged Jimmy, who very much liked to fly (and who also cares about ordinary citizens). So he deregulated the airlines, thus creating countless jobs and bringing true competition—leading to lower prices for consumers—to this vital industry. Now, middle-class Americans can fly to other parts of the country and around the world without having to break the bank. The Man From Plains brought Americans and citizens of the world together by making it easier—and cheaper—to fly.

Thank you, Jimmy.

HE (WITH ROSALYNN) MADE IT EXCITING TO GROW OLD.

In 1987, only a few years out of the White House, Jimmy and Rosalynn got together and wrote *Everything to Gain: Making the Most of the Rest of Your Life.* In doing so they reminded Americans that getting older could turn out to be the best years of their lives. "It is possible to have an entirely different career after our first one has ended and even to weave two or three exciting vocations together, while our ancestors were lucky to survive into what we now think of as middle age," they wrote. Live long and prosper, indeed!

Thank you, Jimmy (and Rosalynn).

HE'S WRITTEN A LOT OF BOOKS.

Jimmy has authored over 30 books. His work has even made the *New York Times*'s bestseller list. He has published political memoirs, collections of his poetry and church lessons, and a novel, and repeatedly has opened his life and experiences to millions through his writings. The Man From Plains has also been the subject of too many books to list here. Some of them are good, some are bad; some are laudatory, some are not. Luckily, Jimmy has his own library in Atlanta to house all those books!

Thank you, Jimmy.

55

HE'S REFUSED TO SIT ON CORPORATE BOARDS OR TAKE MONEY FOR SPEECHES.

Like his hero Harry Truman, Jimmy has never believed a former president should sell himself to the highest bidder. Both he and Harry believed that amassing corporate board memberships and seeking profit for private companies thanks to their fame demeans the presidency. So Jimmy passed on receiving the millions of dollars today's ex-presidents often take for granted. It just wasn't for him. As he has done throughout his life, Jimmy puts principle above profit. He makes his money the hard way: He pays his bills by writing books—and without ghostwriters!

Thank you, Jimmy.

HE NORMALIZED RELATIONS WITH CHINA.

After Richard Nixon famously visited China and shook hands with Communist leader Zhou Enlai, Jimmy had to fine-tune the details of America's new relations with the Asian giant. In 1979, Chinese Vice Premier Deng Xiaoping was the guest of honor at a White House dinner. As always, Jimmy showed class when he arranged the event: He made sure that former president Nixon was on hand. Tricky Dick, after all, had made the night possible by risking a visit to China only a few years earlier.

Thank you, Jimmy (and Richard Nixon).

HE CALLS FOR SEX EDUCATION FOR YOUNG AMERICANS.

Jimmy has never let his own personal religious views on issues like abortion stand in the way of sound public policy. For instance, he believes strongly in providing our children with proper education about sex. Jimmy is more realistic than many of his fellow politicos. "There is now adequate government funding for sex education, but unfortunately it is quite often tied to a legal prohibition against any mention of contraception, despite the fact that a strong majority of American teenagers report having sex before they are 18," he wrote.

For calling it like it is: Thank you, Jimmy.

HE'S FISHED IN SOME REALLY COOL PLACES.

Ever since he was a kid, Jimmy likes to fish. He and Rosalynn learned the ins and outs of fly-fishing and have wrested more than a few fish in their day. But in doing so, they never forget their mission, even when the fish are biting. Once, for example, on a salmon-fishing trip to British Columbia, they took time to learn about the culture, concerns, and history of the Indigenous peoples who lived there. Not many foreign visitors take the trouble to do so. But the Man From Plains and his First Lady did.

Thank you, Jimmy (and Rosalynn).

59

HE AND ROSALYNN OFTEN APPEAR ON THE ATLANTA BRAVES' KISS CAM.

Jimmy and Rosalynn like nothing better than taking in an Atlanta Braves home game. They have been there for the Braves through thick and thin. And every once in a while, they've been caught on the Braves' famous Kiss Cam, smooching. When they kiss, thousands cheer. As a result, the fans leave happy—even if the Braves have lost on the field below. Jimmy has always loved baseball, and in particular he cherishes the fact that he was in the stands when the legendary Hank Aaron hit his 715th home run. (No word, however, if he ever kissed Hank.)

Thank you, Jimmy (and Rosalynn)—and keep on kissing.

HE LEARNED TO DOWNHILL SKI.

Jimmy grew up in the Deep South, where snow isn't, well, exactly abundant. As a result, he was in his 60s before he beheld a pair of downhill skis. And he loved what he saw. Jimmy took up the sport and has mastered some of America's toughest slopes. Sometimes at Christmas he'd take the entire Carter family—and that's a lot of people these days!—on skiing holidays. Jimmy keeps showing seniors that age means nothing if you put your mind—and body!—to it.

Thank you, Jimmy.

HE'S A GUN OWNER WHO CAN'T STAND THE NRA.

Jimmy has been hunting his entire life—but has no time for the NRA. The Man From Plains owns a lot of guns. "I use them carefully, for harvesting game from our woods and fields and during an occasional foray to hunt with my family and friends in other places. But many of us who participate in outdoor sports are dismayed by some of the more extreme policies of the NRA."

Jimmy calls out NRA members for what many of them really are: an insult to the thousands of innocent lives lost to gun violence each year in America.

Thank you, Jimmy.

HE FIGHTS FOR EQUAL RIGHTS FOR WOMEN.

When he was president, Jimmy appointed more women to important posts than any of the chief executives before him. As the son of Miss Lillian and the husband of Rosalynn, he knows full well that he had nothing to fear from strong women and that no man did. As later presidents discovered, when women are in an administration, they usually get the job done better than most men. In 2014, Jimmy even published a book, *A Call to Action: Women, Religion, Violence, and Power,* as part of his life-long efforts to promote women's rights.

Thank you, Jimmy.

HE CARRIED HIS OWN SUITCASES AS PRESIDENT.

Before he became president, Jimmy had always carried his own luggage when traveling. He believed things should be no different—even though he now glided through the skies on Air Force One. And sure enough, Americans began seeing their chief executive hauling his own suitcases! It made headlines across the country. To Jimmy, however, it was just the way things should be— president or not. Although some of his opponents made fun of the Man From Plains, Jimmy knew that, in the end, presidents are not above anyone else.

Thank you, Jimmy.

64

HE LIVED IN PUBLIC HOUSING.

When you visit Plains, there is one stop you simply have to make: Public Housing Unit 9A. It has a large historic plaque on it to remind the world that the future president of the United States and his family, when they faced tough economic times, needed public assistance. Like millions today, they lived in a subsidized unit until they could get back on their feet. The Carter family needed a hand up, not a handout—and they've more than repaid the government for what they received. We should all take note during these challenging times: Their perseverance paid off.

Thank you, Jimmy (and family).

HE WATCHED *ALL THE PRESIDENT'S MEN* IN THE WHITE HOUSE.

Only weeks after moving into the White House, less than three years after President Nixon resigned, Jimmy watched *All the President's Men,* then all the rage in America. The 1976 film chronicles the unraveling of the Nixon presidency and the dishonesty of one of Jimmy's predecessors. While Jimmy needed no lessons in ethical behavior, it is interesting that this was the first movie he watched as president. The Man From Plains, thank goodness, was no Richard Nixon.

Thank you, Jimmy.

66

HE CAN PLAY THE UKULELE.

Jimmy knows how to play only one instrument: the ukulele. He perfected his performances while he and Rosalynn lived in Hawaii (and when no one was really watching). Later in life he donated trees harvested from his property in Plains so that a whole new line of ukuleles could be designed. In doing so, Jimmy exemplified sustainable harvesting practices. At one point, Pearl Jam's Eddie Vedder even performed using one of the Jimmy-brand ukuleles, and he and Jimmy raised a lot of money for charity! Well done, gentlemen.

Thank you, Jimmy (and Eddie).

HE ALERTED THE WORLD TO THE DANGERS OF KILLER RABBITS.

Not since the 1975 cult classic *Monty Python and the Holy Grail* had the reality of killer rabbits been brought to the world's attention so dramatically until the Man From Plains came along. President Jimmy was in a boat when the ferocious rabbit made its move. A lot of people made fun of him for describing the assault—but legions of *Holy Grail* fans were on his side. They understood, just as Jimmy did, that Killer Rabbits can deliver much more than a flesh wound….

Thank you, Jimmy.

HE APPOINTED MORE AFRICAN AMERICANS AND LATINOS TO THE BENCH THAN EVER BEFORE.

Jimmy believes that the judges in our courts should reflect America's demographics. To help make this a reality, he asked his people to get him the best African-American and Latino (and female) candidates they could find for him to appoint when he held America's top job. And find them they did. Jimmy's appointees brought him and the courts great credit. By the time Jimmy left office in 1981, he had appointed more minority and women judges than all his predecessors combined. The courts have never been the same. And that's a good thing.

Thank you, Jimmy.

HE'S A CARPENTER.

When he left the White House, Jimmy's personal staff gave him a going-away present: a woodworking set. When he got back home to Plains, Jimmy headed to his workshop. Over the years, he's made, with his own hands, everything from tables and rocking chairs to church collection plates and everything in between. Jimmy often auctions off his masterpieces to raise money for his many worthy causes. Eventually, the Man From Plains gave his famous woodworking tools to one of his grandsons—and that young man has already done wonders with them.

Thank you, Jimmy.

HE CUTS THE LAWN AT HIS CHURCH.

Just because you're a former president doesn't mean you can get out of helping your local church like all the other members of the congregation do! That's why over the years many visitors to Plains have come across the 39th president pushing a lawnmower on the grounds of his tiny Baptist church. This sends an important message for sure, but beyond all that: The Man From Plains is so good at it, he rarely uses a trimmer. And if you've been to Maranatha, you know just how much lawn the Man From Plains has had to cut: a lot!

Thank you, Jimmy.

HE GREETS EACH PASSENGER ON THE FLIGHTS HE TAKES.

A funny thing has happened to hundreds—if not thousands—of passengers on airplanes in recent years. Just as the flight gets underway, a U.S. president comes down the aisle greeting everyone onboard. While other former presidents stay hidden up in first class, Jimmy visits with the people on every single flight he takes and has posed for thousands of pictures with ordinary Americans high in the sky. This shouldn't surprise anyone, however: The Man From Plains has always been a man of the people.

Thank you, Jimmy.

HE WHIPPED TED KENNEDY'S ASS.

While the late Ted Kennedy was a liberal icon and a great American, he could also be, well, a jerk. He showed this big-time when he challenged Jimmy, a sitting Democratic president, for their party's nomination. Which meant that the Man From Plains had to spend months preparing for and fighting a challenge when he could have been sparring with Republicans. But Jimmy didn't waver and showed he was no pushover, even telling a group of Congressmen he'd "whip Ted's ass." And he did. The Man From Plains caught grief for his salty language—but he kept the nomination.

Thank you, Jimmy.

ON HIS FIRST DAY AS GEORGIA'S GOVERNOR, HE ANNOUNCED THAT OFFICIAL RACISM WAS OVER.

On Jimmy's first day as governor of Georgia, way back in 1971, he shocked many of the good ol' boys (and gals) in his state, and across the entire South, right out of the starting gate. "The time for racial discrimination is over," he said firmly and proudly in his first speech on the job. No governor had ever said anything like that before. By doing so, Jimmy announced to the country and the world that a new era dawned. And although his father had been a segregationist and little Jimmy had attended an all-white school, Governor Carter knew the right thing to do.

Thank you, Jimmy.

HE APPOINTED A PRESIDENTIAL COMMISSION ON MENTAL HEALTH.

Before Jimmy arrived in Washington, mental health was rarely ever mentioned in politics. But even if Jimmy had wanted to ignore the issue, that would have been impossible: He was married to Rosalynn. She'd been fighting for mental health reform and understanding since the early 1960s. There was no way she'd stop just because she was now living in the White House. Jimmy named Rosalynn head of the new presidential commission and the veil soon lifted on discussing mental health issues. This changed the lives of millions who now knew their president understood and cared.

Thank you, Jimmy (and Rosalynn).

HE MADE IT SAFER TO DRIVE.

Jimmy started driving when he was around 10 years old. In rural Georgia, that's just what you did back then. When he became president, the Man From Plains knew driving had to be made safer for drivers and passengers alike. Too many Americans were dying on the roads and highways each year. So Jimmy got to work and authorized regulations forcing big automakers to install seat belts and airbags in all new vehicles. By conservative estimates, seat belts and airbags save almost 10,000 American lives every year.

Thank you, Jimmy (and drivers everywhere thank you, too).

HE DIDN'T GET SEDUCED BY BOB WOODWARD.

It is a Washington rite of passage for presidents to drop their guard and give access to the *Washington Post*'s Bob Woodward (of Watergate fame). As history has shown, bromances with Bob (one of the finest journalists of his generation) seldom end well for the occupant of the Oval Office. But Jimmy knew better. While he and Bob know each other and have talked many times (and have had a few dustups along the way), Jimmy never fell for the Woodward hug. And so Jimmy has been able to write his own story.

Thank you, Jimmy (and sorry, Bob).

HE SET AN EXAMPLE BY WALKING THE PARADE ROUTE ON INAUGURATION DAY.

On January 20, 1977, after being sworn in and delivering his inaugural address, Jimmy (along with Rosalynn and their children) did something no modern president had ever done: He got out of the presidential limo and walked the parade route back to the White House while spectators cheered and cheered. He said later that he hoped his gesture might have encouraged more Americans to get physically fit. More importantly perhaps, it also reminded Americans that their new president was, quite simply, one of them.

Thank you, Jimmy.

HIS FAMOUS SMILE.

Not since Franklin Roosevelt has any President had such a winning smile. Jimmy has been showing us those famous molars of his for decades, and none of us are tired of them. That's why American cartoonists miss the Man From Plains living in the White House: His was—and is still—the greatest, most dazzling presidential smile to draw. Jimmy may be a bit older now, but his smile still dazzles and brings us all hope.

Thank you, Jimmy.

Jimmy with his long-time friend Jill Stuckey modeling Jimmy Carter smile masks in Plains.

HE PERFORMED WITH DIZZY GILLESPIE.

As president, Jimmy wanted to highlight musicians and musical genres never celebrated at the White House before. So on June 18, 1978, he organized a special jazz concert on the South Lawn of the mansion. One of the musicians he invited was the legendary Dizzy Gillespie. Dizzy closed the show with a special version of his classic "Salt Peanuts." No surprise, but Dizzy insisted that President Jimmy come on stage and sing the two-word chorus, "Salt Peanuts!" The Man From Plains agreed. Even Dizzy was impressed.

Thank you, Jimmy.

HE TURNED DOWN THE HEAT IN THE WHITE HOUSE.

When Jimmy asked Americans to join him in conserving energy, he led by example. In 1977, he asked all citizens to turn down the heat in their homes in aid of this worthy cause. Most were more than happy to do so, especially when Jimmy announced he'd ordered the thermostats in the White House lowered. The Man From Plains dropped the temperature at 1600 Pennsylvania Avenue to 65 degrees. No hypocrite, he. Staff in the president's house, like people everywhere, discovered they could still carry on and be comfortable at 65 degrees.

Thank you, Jimmy.

HE MADE CANADIANS HAPPY BY CORRECTING THE MOVIE *ARGO*.

Jimmy thought Ben Affleck's 2012 movie *Argo,* which dramatized the 1979 rescue of six U.S. hostages from revolutionary Iran, was a good movie. The Americans managed to find refuge in the residence of Canada's ambassador to Iran, Ken Taylor. However, Jimmy felt that the Hollywood version didn't do justice to America's Canadian neighbors. "Ninety percent of the contributions to the ideas and the consummation of the plan was Canadian," Carter told CNN. "And the movie gives almost full credit to the American CIA." As a result, Canadians cheered Carter at his next appearance in their country and Affleck added a new ending that provided more information on Canada and on Ken Taylor's heroism.

Thank you, Jimmy (and Ambassador Taylor).

President Carter in the Oval Office on February 1, 1980, with the six American diplomats that Canadian officials bravely helped spirit out of revolutionary Iran.

HE'S WRITTEN THOUSANDS OF HANDWRITTEN NOTES TO THOSE WHO HAVE WRITTEN TO HIM.

Over the years, thousands upon thousands of ordinary people from America and across the globe have written to Jimmy. He's always appreciated that. In fact he often writes handwritten greetings in the margins of the letters sent his way and mails them back to the writer. He started doing this many years ago. The Man From Plains has also been known to correct his epistoler's grammar—shades of Miss Julia Coleman! Most importantly, he's made it a priority to send handwritten notes—sometimes signing them "Love, Jimmy"—to the American children who write to him. There are a lot of happy kids out there.

Thank you, Jimmy.

To Art: Thanks very much,
I'll retain Megan's article
so we can share it —
Best wishes,
Jimmy Carter

HE CONVINCED GARTH BROOKS AND TRISHA YEARWOOD TO BUILD HOUSES FOR THE POOR.

For more than a decade, musical superstars Garth Brooks and Trisha Yearwood have spent a week every year building houses for the poor through Habitat for Humanity. Working in tandem with Jimmy and Rosalynn, their star power has raised the profile of Habitat far and wide. But it's likely they would have never heard of Habitat if it hadn't been for the former president.

Thank you, Jimmy (and Rosalynn, Garth, and Trisha).

HE WROTE A BOOK ABOUT HIS MOTHER.

We all love our moms. But Jimmy took this one step further when it came to the redoubtable Miss Lillian: In 2008 he published *A Remarkable Mother*. Thus he was able to share with us his many stories about his mother, including the time she joined the Peace Corps in her 70s and moved to India! She also liked to appear on *The Tonight Show Starring Johnny Carson*. More importantly, Miss Lillian often defied segregation-era rules when few dared do so. If she didn't deserve a book, I don't know who does.

Thank you, Jimmy (and Miss Lillian).

HE'S NEITHER RIGHT NOR LEFT.

While many have tried over many decades, it's really hard to put Jimmy in a political box. He leans right on certain issues and left on others. In fact, he reflects where most Americans stand on almost all issues. But above all else, Jimmy believes you should always listen carefully to the arguments from the other side.

He believes, in short, in an advanced American democracy. Given our divisive political climate, that's a pretty good belief to have.

Thank you, Jimmy.

HE'S BEEN ON
THE TONIGHT SHOW.

Though he's always tried to go to bed early (after all, he usually gets up at 5 a.m.!), Jimmy is no stranger to late-night television. In fact, he's made more appearances on *The Tonight Show* than any other president: Since leaving the White House, he's made over 10 guest appearances.

"*Heeeee*re's Jimmy!"

Thank you, Jimmy.

HE WAS THE FIRST PRESIDENT TO WELCOME A POPE TO WASHINGTON.

Before Jimmy and Rosalynn moved into 1600 Pennsylvania Avenue, no pope had ever visited the White House or Washington itself. Jimmy changed all that. On October 6, 1979, Pope John Paul II dropped by for a chat that Jimmy had arranged. The pontiff was very pleased with his visit. "It gives me great joy to be the first pope in history to come to the capital of this nation, and I thank almighty God for this blessing," his holiness said on the White House lawn. The Baptist and the Catholic had done a good thing.

Thank you, Jimmy (and Pope John Paul II).

HE FOUGHT THE FEDERAL DEFICIT AT EVERY TURN.

Unlike his successors, Democrats and Republicans alike, President Jimmy did all he could to lower America's debt. In fact, he told liberal Democrats from Congress in his administration's earliest days that one of his priorities was to put the country in surplus by the end of his first term. Ronald Reagan and his Republicans told the country in 1980 that Jimmy was a wild-spending liberal. Once elected, however, the Gipper and his crew cranked up the deficit to a record high by cutting taxes for rich Americans at the expense of the poor. The Man From Plains would have never done that.

Thank you, Jimmy.

HE HAD BREAKFAST WITH MAYOR PETE AND HIS HUSBAND IN PLAINS.

When Mayor Pete (who is now the secretary of transportation) was running for president, he needed advice from a winner. So he and his husband traveled to Plains to have breakfast with Jimmy and Rosalynn. The four of them had a great time. What? An openly gay American political leader, along with his husband, the first gentleman of South Bend, Chasten Glezman, sharing a president's table in small-town America? This was a historic moment for all those who fight for equal rights for same-sex couples.

Thank you, Jimmy (and Rosalynn, Secretary Pete, and Chasten).

LIKE HARRY TRUMAN, HE KNEW WHERE THE BUCK STOPPED.

Jimmy's personal presidential hero is Harry S. Truman of Independence, Missouri. Homespun Harry had been a farmer, too. And just like Jimmy (see his "malaise speech"), Harry never shied away from telling Americans what he thought, even when it would have been better politically to just shut up. If you recall, Harry had a special sign on his Oval Office desk: "*The* BUCK STOPS *here!*"

Jimmy put that sign back.

Thank you, Jimmy.

HE TOOK PHONE CALLS FROM ORDINARY AMERICANS WHILE IN THE OVAL OFFICE.

Jimmy has always been a man of the people. Early on in his presidency he even opened up the phone lines so that ordinary Americans could phone in and ask him questions about government policy and whatever else was on their minds. With news broadcasting legend Walter Cronkite serving as moderator (to make sure no one could claim the calls had been faked), President Jimmy was on the phone for two hours, talking to people like you and me. It was called "Ask President Carter."

This was just another way for Jimmy to bring the presidency closer to the people.

Thank you, Jimmy (and Walter).

HE SALUTED HIS PREDECESSOR IN HIS VERY FIRST WORDS AS PRESIDENT.

Jimmy is a gentleman. He respected his opponents, including the man he ran against in a hard-fought and close campaign in 1976. While he disagreed with President Ford on many issues, Jimmy never saw Ford as an enemy. When writing his inaugural address, Jimmy made sure, right off the top, to recognize Ford's service to America. "For myself and for our nation, I want to recognize my predecessor for all he has done to heal our land," Jimmy said in his first public words as president.

Imagine if all our leaders showed such respect for one another.

Thank you, Jimmy (and Jerry).

HE'S ALWAYS ON TIME.

To say that Jimmy has always been punctual would be an understatement. When he says he'll be somewhere at a certain time, he is. Other presidents (that's you, Bill Clinton) have been chronically late. But not the Man From Plains. Jimmy has always respected the time of all Americans as if it were his own. He is, after all, one of us. Rumor has it, though, that he was late to his own wedding in 1946. Jimmy denies it—and Rosalynn remains silent. But they got to the altar and *that's* what matters!

Thank you, Jimmy.

HE WORE REALLY COOL HAWAIIAN SHIRTS.

Don Ho has nothing on Jimmy. (Admit it, if you're of a certain age, you're now humming the words to "Tiny Bubbles"). When Jimmy was in the Navy, he was stationed in Hawaii. Folks remember him wearing some really cool (and loud!) Hawaiian shirts during that period. And Rosalynn did her part too. "She was the best hula dancer among all the Navy wives," Jimmy says proudly.

Mahalo, Jimmy (and Rosalynn).

HE WROTE SEXY LETTERS TO HIS WIFE.

While Jimmy loved being a U.S. Navy submariner, those long voyages kept him away from his beloved. So he wrote her letters. Many letters. And, well, he was no Baptist prude! "I miss more than anything else your mouth and breasts and body and the way you feel and smell to me when we're making love," he wrote his beloved. Then Jimmy told Rosalynn what mattered even more. "But after a day or so those things become less and less important to me, and I want to touch your hair or look at you across the room."

No wonder they've been happily married for 76 years.

Thank you, Jimmy (and Rosalynn).

HE KNOWS EVERY SQUARE INCH OF THE HOLY LAND.

When Jimmy went into a meeting with a foreign leader, he'd done his homework. For example, before he brought Egypt's Anwar Sadat and Israel's Menachem Begin to Camp David, Jimmy spent hours and days studying maps of the Holy Land. In the end, he got to know the terrain down to the last desert stone. And in the end, he also managed to bring peace to these once-warring nations, saving countless lives.

Thank you, Jimmy.

HE MAKES HIS OWN WINE.

The Carter family of Plains, Georgia, has been making their own wine for 150 years. Today, Jimmy carries on this family tradition, producing about 100 bottles of his famous wine every few years or so. "I've modified the (Carter family) recipe dramatically because in the past the custom was to put an excessive amount of sugar in the grapes," he says. "So, when all of the available sugar changed to alcohol, you had a lot of sugar left over, with a very sweet wine. And so, I've tried to balance by studying French winemaking books and talking to some of the major winemakers."

The Man From Plains often donates bottles of his wine to Carter Center auctions to help him and his team continue their good works.

Thank you, Jimmy. (*Santé!*)

97.5

HE SLEPT OVER AT MY HOUSE.

When Jimmy came to my town in 2012, I invited him for a sleepover. He agreed. So the Man From Plains and his wife slept in my house. Jimmy even planted a ceremonial tree in my garden; it now sports a proud plaque:

"This tree was planted by the 39th President of the United States, the Honorable Jimmy Carter, on November 22, 2012."

His visit was the highest honor of my career.

But there's a downside: Now I can't move! (We'll deal with that when the time comes....)

In the meantime: Thank you, Jimmy.

HE'S JIMMY CARTER.

A hero to countless Americans, Jimmy and his amazing accomplishments continue to influence and inspire.

He remains a shining example of political and moral leadership in this unsettled world of ours.

He anchors the American past, improves its present, and lights the way to the better tomorrows that lie within our collective grasp.

And he's my friend.

Thank you, Jimmy.
And happy birthday!

ACKNOWLEDGMENTS

I first met Laura Carney and Steven Seighman in Plains, Georgia, on a summer weekend in 2017 and we've kept in touch ever since. In early 2022 they planted the idea for this book in my head. This wouldn't have come to fruition without them.

My wife, Alison, knows more about my admiration for the Man From Plains than anyone else, and she loves the Carters too.

Copy editors Michel Pharand and Laura Carney have generously agreed not to divulge how many errors they found in my early draft. Steven Seighman did wonders with the design of the volume. My dear friend in Plains, Jill Stuckey, went out of her way to help with photographs, as did Erica Cotton Boyce at Habitat for Humanity; Betsy Theroux, director, House Media Services Office and house messenger at the Georgia Legislature; the distinguished historian Steven Hochman at The Carter Center; and Tony Clark at the Jimmy Carter Presidential Library.

It is a great pleasure to recognize and express my gratitude to my fellow Canadian, Dan Aykroyd, for his assistance with *98 Reasons to Thank Jimmy Carter*. Mr. Aykroyd is a very serious student of political history and I owe him a great deal. His longtime assistant, Lisa Garelick, also merits my thanks.

Most of all, I extend my heartfelt thanks to a special couple I am deeply honored to call my friends: Jimmy and Rosalynn Carter of Plains, Georgia. They have made our world a better place and, by extending their friendship to me, have made me a better man.

ABOUT THE AUTHOR

Photo by Bernard Clark

ARTHUR MILNES is a nationally recognized presidential historian whose previous books include studies of presidents George H.W. Bush, Jimmy Carter, and Franklin Roosevelt. A journalist and political speechwriter, he writes frequently about the lives and legacies of the presidents of the United States.